## Dedicated to:

*My loving parents and two sisters*

*Those I call my friends.*
*You are a continuous source*
*of growth and support.*

*The Kennedy Fowler Clinic*

*The Windsor Express*

*The University of Ottawa*


**A to Z**

# CHAPTER 1

Bounce ... bounce ... bounce ... bounce ...

Clyde McCall always has his basketball with him. He dribbles it while watching television. He dribbles it before going to bed. He even dribbles it on his way to the bathroom. Every morning he practices a variety of dribble moves on his way to school. Clyde dreams of one day being a professional basketball player.

When he arrives at the classroom door, he is sure to place the ball in a safe place. Then he gets his homework ready for class.

Today, Clyde looks up and spots his best friends coming down the hall.

Clyde gets a big hug from Maria Clara Reynolds, nicknamed "MC Reynolds," and then greets Jacob Grant, nicknamed "Jakes," with their "special" handshake. Lastly, but far from least, his best friend Marlon Walters sees the group and runs up behind Clyde and taps him on his left shoulder. Clyde looks that way, and Marlon appears on his right, laughing hysterically.

As they walk into class together, Clyde notices Marlon is holding a picture of the newest basketball shoes from *B-Ball World Magazine*.

Clyde looks down at his old sneakers, and then he stares at Marlon's picture of the basketball shoes. Clyde's shoes were pretty beat up; it is hard to even tell what color they are anymore. The laces do not help. They used to be white, now they are light brown. The soles of the shoes are wearing thin, giving Clyde no grip. When Clyde walks he feels the grooves made in the shoe from his toes, as well as the hole that's forming where his left big toe is. Clyde can't help but feel a little jealous of Marlon and embarrassed about the condition of his shoes.

Marlon stands there chuckling and says, "You like these, don't you, Clyde. I got a discount on them in the all-black, spaceship editions. They're on the way."

Clyde looks at Marlon's picture of his new shoes with puppy-dog, sad eyes as the class bell rings.

Clyde takes his seat in class as Mr. Paul, his homeroom teacher, gives the introduction to the year's final assignment. Soon, Mr. Paul starts the first lesson of the day—math.

Before Clyde knows it, he is daydreaming about the shoes he wants and how amazing he will play if he has them. He imagines himself moving and changing directions like Kyrie Irving, shooting like Steph Curry, and scoring like Damian Lillard. Mr. Paul says, "Hey, Clyde, what's the answer to this math problem?" Clyde, snapping out of his daydream, nervously answers incorrectly.

At the end of class, Mr. Paul stops Clyde in the hallway and asks to speak to him privately in his classroom.

Mr. Paul says, "Clyde, you have to pay attention in class and be a example for the other students."

Clyde says, "I know, Mr. Paul, but I have a big game coming up, and I need new shoes. I have a big responsibility, you know."

Mr. Paul laughs, smiles at Clyde and says, "No, Clyde, you don't have any real responsibilities, not just yet, but one day you will. You're a good kid, Clyde. I'm sure if you ask your parents, they'll help with your shoe problem. Have a good rest of your day!"

inspiration

- HOMEWORK DUE THURS
- TEST ON MON
- FIELDTRIP NEXT TUE

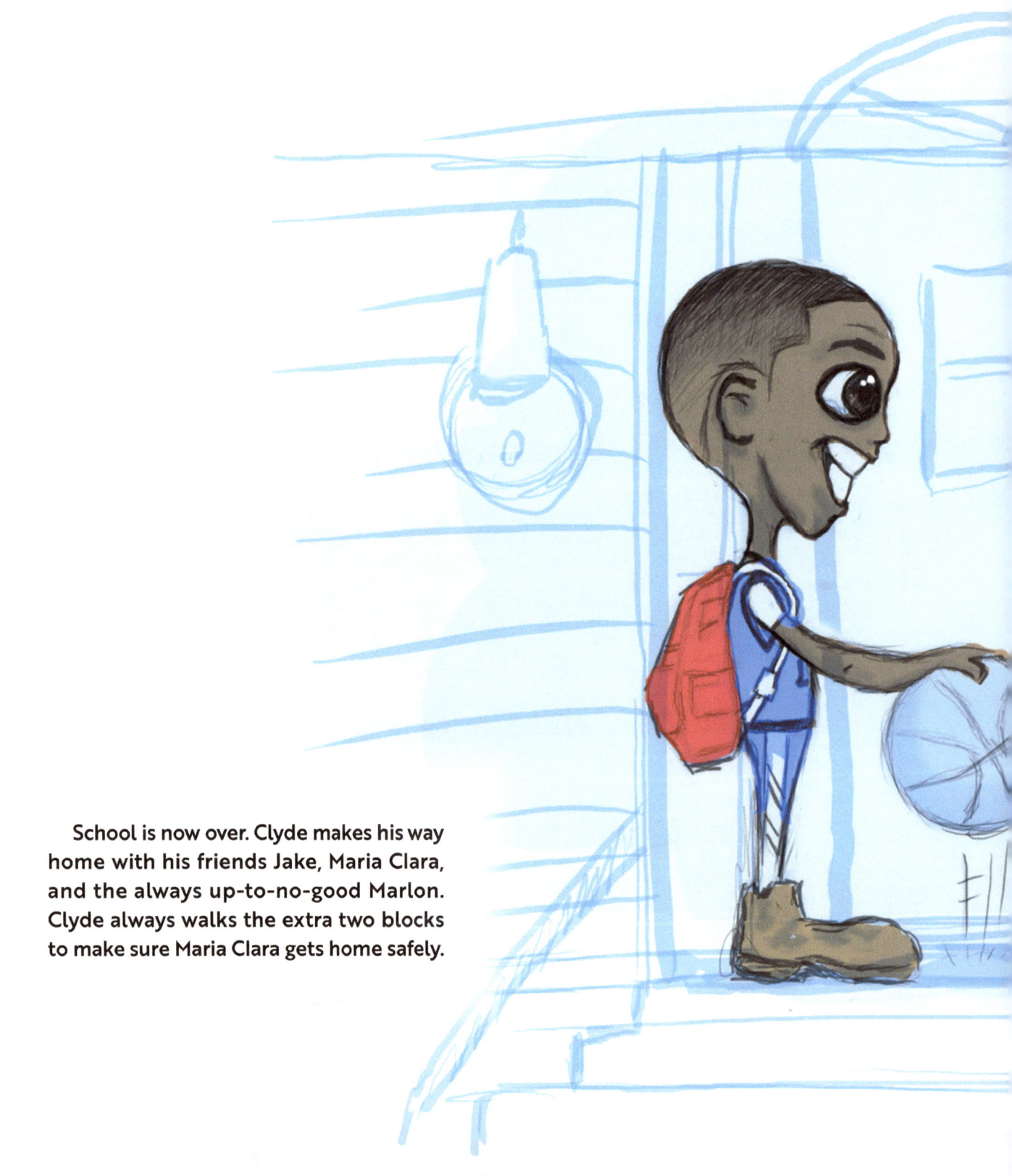

School is now over. Clyde makes his way home with his friends Jake, Maria Clara, and the always up-to-no-good Marlon. Clyde always walks the extra two blocks to make sure Maria Clara gets home safely.

## CHAPTER 2

Clyde arrives at home and sees there are no cars in the driveway. He enters the house. He tiptoes up the steps to his room to change and, even more carefully, tiptoes back down as he tries to sneak out before his mom can hear him.

Just before he gets to the door he hears a voice ... his mother's: "Excuse me, where do you think you're going, young man?"

"But ... but ... but I have the Forest City Championship in two days, Mom. I need to practice," says Clyde.

"No buts, Clyde Andrew McCall. You know the rules. If you want to play basketball, you must do your homework first, AND let me check it."

"Okay, Mom," Clyde says with a sad face.

Clyde does his homework, and his mother checks it. He eats dinner, and then goes to practice outside until the streetlights come on. Clyde later hears, "It's time for bed, Clyde. One last shot and go shower." It's his mother, shouting from the window. Clyde knows that is his one and only warning.

# CHAPTER 3

Clyde, now in bed, falls asleep and has a terrible nightmare about the Forest City Championship. He is on a fast break and his old shoelaces have come undone. He steps on one of the laces, trips, falls, and watches the ball go out of bounds and his team loses the game. Clyde wakes up in a panic, determined to get these new basketball shoes for when he plays in the Forest City Championship.

Clyde wants to ask his parents to buy him the shoes that Marlon showed him, but he knows his mother and father will probably say, "You know growing up, all I had was one pair of shoes for everything. You don't need another pair. You just want one. And we can't always get what we want in this world."

He says to himself, "It's hopeless."

While Clyde is eating his breakfast, a light bulb goes off in his head. He knows just the person to go to: Maria Clara. Her brother is the manager at the local sports store.

As he dribbles to school, Clyde stops at the convenience store to buy Maria Clara's favorite candy bar, the double chocolate Wayyve bar with the caramel filling. He is really excited to see Maria Clara to ask her about the basketball shoes. When he spots Maria in the hallway, at the usual meeting spot, he's extra friendly as he gives her the Wayyve Bar. "Hey Marrriiiaaaaa Clara, how ya dooooiiinnggg?" Clyde says with a soft, innocent tone.

MC stares at Clyde with a smirk and says: "Hah! I was wondering when you'd come to me. You've come to the right person, Clyde. I can help you, my friend, but it'll cost yah." She winks. Clyde has a feeling he is in for more walks home with his friend.

"I brought you your favorite chocolate bar. The one you always eat with the caramel filling. Isn't that enough?" asks Clyde.

"No, it is not. I'm a busy girl these days and you need my help. I'll do you this favor, but in return I'll need your Fran's Aquarium & Arcade pass for a month, *and* you will bring me a Wayyve Bar every other day for the rest of the week. And make sure it's the one with the caramel on the inside. Lastly, be sure to tell the other kids who helped with your shoes. That's good for business," she says with a big smile.

Clyde's mouth drops open. "Seriously, a month?" he asks.

"Yup, one whole month. And I will need your arcade tokens, too. It's the cost of doing business," replies Maria.

"Fine, I accept your offer," Clyde says hesitantly. His need for the shoes is greater than his love for his arcade tokens or the cost of the Wayyve Bars.

Clyde has no choice but to agree. He has to have those shoes.

# CHAPTER 4

It is the day before the game. Jacob has come up with an idea for the year-end school project. While in class, Jacob asks Mr. Paul if he can make a mini-movie about the Forest City Championship game for his creative assignment. The mini-movie, he explains, will be like the videos made in the NBA.

Mr. Paul agrees and lets Jacob record the game, edit the film, and share it on YouTube.

Mr. Paul asks Jacob why he wants to create a mini-movie.

Jacob says to Mr. Paul, "I want to show my friends to the world. The world needs to know we exist."

Mr. Paul smiles like a proud father. He recognizes Jacob's love for his friends and that he wants to help inspire others through sports.

# CHAPTER 5

Clyde meets Maria Clara at the usual spot outside of class before the bell. She's holding a rectangular box. She gets closer, opens it, and there are Clyde's all-white basketball shoes. Clyde's eyes light up. He can hear the angels singing and see the light of heaven beaming through that box. His prayers have been answered. Clyde has never seen anything so beautiful. He cannot stop staring at the shiny sneakers. He takes the shoes with their metallic silver tongues out of the box and places them on his feet, ever so gently. As he ties the laces, Clyde feels the sole of the shoes on his feet. There are no holes. It is love at first sight for young Clyde McCall.

# CHAPTER 6

This afternoon, St. Anthony is playing their rival Green Oaks public school. St. Anthony has an impressive 14-5 record and plays stellar team defense. Green Oaks has had a record season of 18-1. Leading the way is dominant center Jerami Jerreau. He is bigger than the other kids his age and very skilled. This will be a very tough game for St. Anthony.

Sitting front row, MC Reynolds, Jakes, and the up-to-no-good Marlon are cheering the team on. After the first quarter, Marlon sneaks into the secretary's office. He looks in the school directory for Clyde's parents' work numbers and calls them both. He pretends to be the school nurse and tells them Clyde has had an accident, and that they should come to the school right away!

Clyde's parents arrive at the school together in a panic. They check the nursing area. Nobody is there. Clyde's father hears loud noises coming from the gym. When they open the gym doors, they see Clyde dribbling up the court on a fast break and scoring two points.

It's the beginning of the fourth quarter. The two teams have been trading baskets but Green Oaks has been winning the majority of the game. Clyde aggressively defends the opposing team's point guard, preventing him from dribbling up the court easily. STEAL! Clyde adds two more points to the score. As the game goes on, St. Anthony continues to play excellent defense.

There is one minute and thirty seconds left in the game. Clyde gets a pass and dribbles hard to the basket. He is fouled and shoots two free throws. Everyone knows who the ball is going to - Jerami Jerreau. He flies by his defender and scores with ease.

St Anthony calls a timeout. They need a plan to win the game. They come out of the timeout ready to execute. Clyde makes a beautiful pass to his teammate who scores two points.

The score is now 43-42.

Green Oaks calls a timeout.

Jerami Jerreau receives the ball again; only this time he doesn't see Clyde sneaking up behind him to steal the ball.

St. Anthony is down one point. The ball is in the hands of Clyde McCall. As Clyde dribbles up the court, he looks up at the clock and sees there are six seconds left in the game. He fakes left, dribbles right, then shoots the basketball.

Mr. McCall yells just before Clyde shoots the ball, "THAT'S MY BOY! IT'S YOUR TIME NOW, SON!!"

**SWISHHHH! TWO POINTS.
GAME OVER.**

After he scores the basket, Clyde screams with joy and excitement. "WE DID IT! WE DID IT! WE WON THE FOREST CITY CHAMPIONSHIP! WE ARE THE CHAMPS!!"

Clyde takes his first-place medal and runs over to his parents with his arms open. "Hey, Momma. Hey, Dad, did you see that shot?! That was for you. I've been practicing that shot outside on the net. SWISH!! That's why I needed the shoes. You see now. It's the shoes. They're the reason I did it, Momma."

Clyde's mother looks at him with a glowing, proud smile and says to him, "Clyde, we love you. We are so proud of you, my son. But it was not the shoes. It was you. Look at your shoes, Clyde," she says. Clyde looks at his brand-new all-white shoes to see they are not so white anymore. They have scuff marks on them from the game.

"It was your practice and your will. You are strong. And you showed everyone here today what you have inside of you. Remember that your game comes from within".

They leave the gym, champions forever. Clyde's mother taught him a valuable lesson that day. The value of himself.

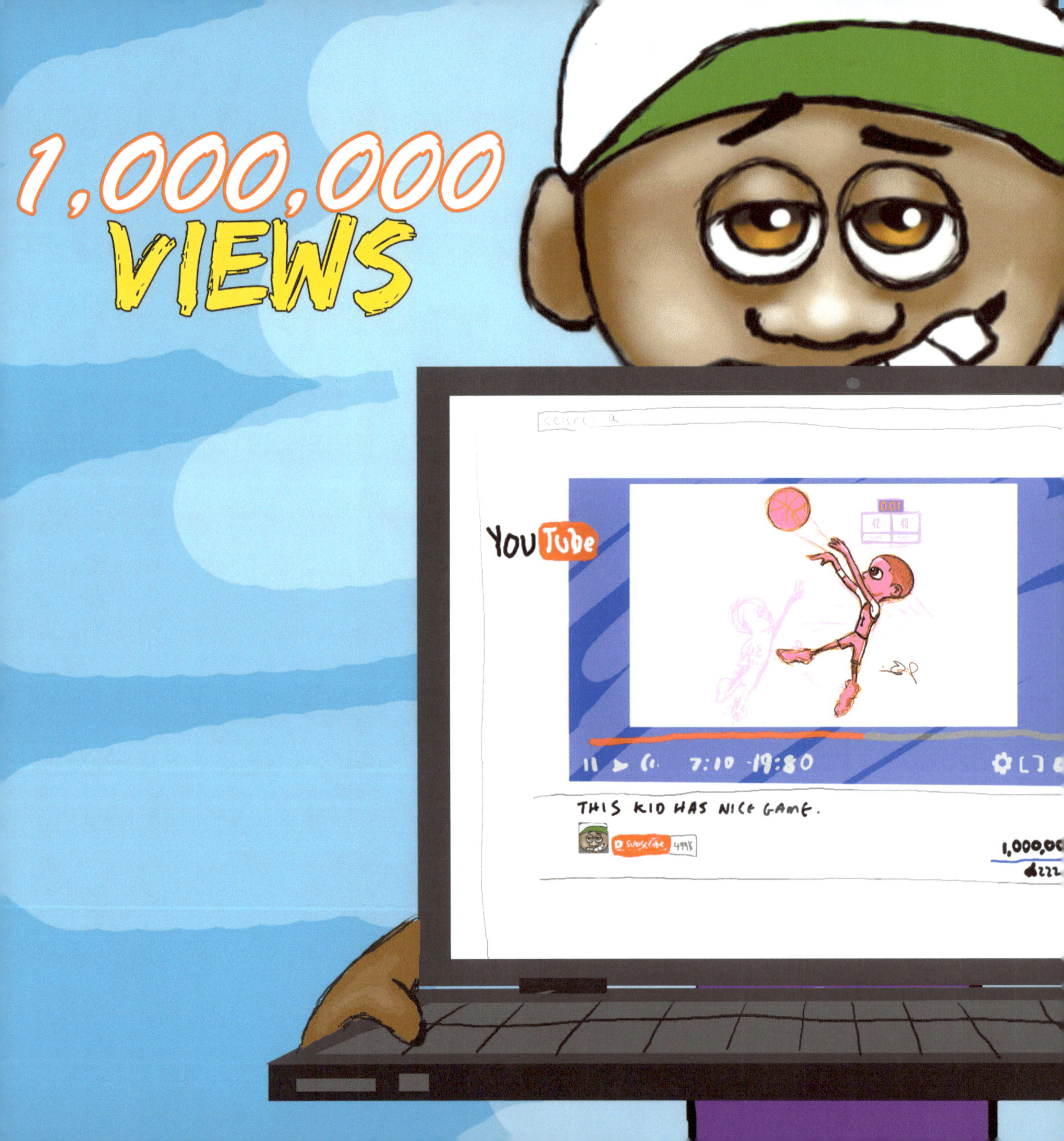
1,000,000
VIEWS
YouTube
7:10 -19:80
THIS KID HAS NICE GAME.

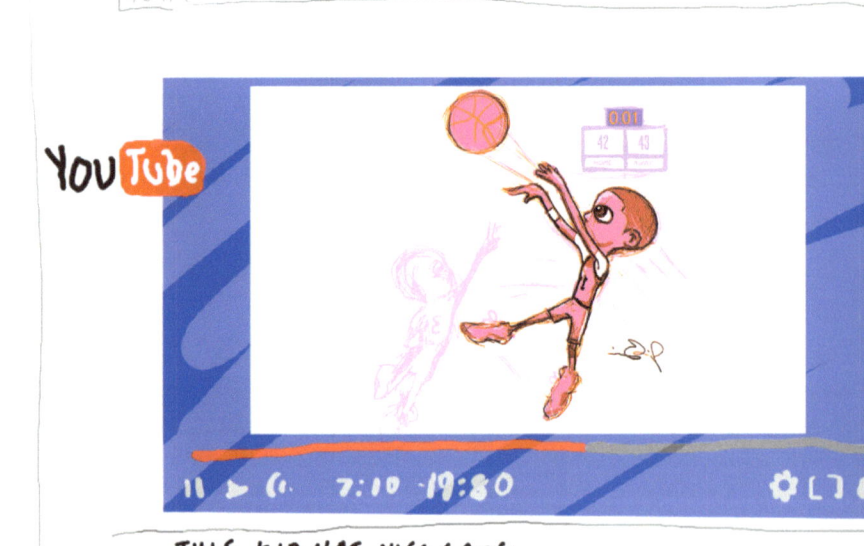

The next day at school Clyde finds out that Jacob's recording was viewed over one million times on YouTube. Jacob would receive an A+ for his creative year-end assignment. The school now records all sporting events as a way to encourage positive activity.

Word spreads around the school, thanks to Clyde, about Maria Clara's helping hand in getting Clyde the shoes. She knows she is on to something, once the other kids start coming her way with "special requests." There will be lots of Wayyve Bars in the future for young MC Reynolds.

## CHAPTER 7

When Marlon is invited over to Clyde's house for dinner the next evening, he receives an earful from Mrs. McCall.

Mrs. McCall explains to Marlon that he could have caused serious trouble for herself and Mr. McCall at their work with his stunt.

Marlon responds by saying, "I'm so sorry, ma'am, but what good is the game if Clyde's number one fans can't watch?"

Mr. and Mrs. McCall know Marlon has made a good point.

After dinner, Marlon returns home and Clyde goes outside to practice.

Clyde is happy about the game-winning shot for weeks. He and his mother make a deal. Now, for good luck, Clyde always does his homework before going outside to practice.

THE END.

# Acknowledgements

*You helped inspire possibility and
the idea to follow through with creativity.
Thank you, Paul Riley.*

*Jermaine Baylis, you brought the story to life*

# Note from the author

*Carpe diem.*

The Quest of Clyde McCall
Copyright © 2018 by Warren Ward

No part of this publication may be reproduced, distributed, or transmitted in any form or by any means, including photocopying, recording, or other electronic or mechanical methods, without the prior written permission of the author, except in the case of brief quotations embodied in critical reviews and certain other non-commercial uses permitted by copyright law.

Tellwell Talent
www.tellwell.ca

ISBN
978-1-77370-701-3 (Hardcover)
978-1-77370-700-6 (Paperback)
978-1-77370-702-0 (eBook)